# Preface

Throughout history, moments arise when societies stand at the crossroads of change, and at this still early stage of a new millennium, change is beckoning to us. It is within these transformative junctures that a new ideology, Adho-Societalism, finds its place. This book seeks to explore and elucidate the principles of this new ideology, offering a fresh perspective on how we can transform our world for the better.

Adho-Societalism is a response to a crisis that stems from the prioritization of competition and profit over cooperation and people by governments and societies. It aims to build a world where everyone can succeed by prioritizing values like fairness and justice, which modern societies throw to the side. Adho-Societalism offers a positive vision for the future by creating a society where everyone can thrive and contribute.

# Preamble

Across the world, a harsh reality has manifested of ever-increasing capital for those who have the means to produce seized from those who don't. This is the natural disposition of humanity, perfected and refined over the ages. However, while we as a species cannot escape greed, we can escape its ever-looming and seemingly perpetual grip on society. Yet to do so, we must escape our dualistic idea of politics. Conservative and unfettered free-market rule stands on one side, while the leftist, planned state with an all-powerful regime unrestricted by the market stands on the other. All else in between these two ideas of governance is the political spectrum that we know now.

However, while all political systems address the material concerns of the people, none take action in a way that serves the whole society. Systems such as communism propose eliminating the wealthy and aim to abolish social and economic competition in favor of predetermined outcomes decided by the state. Other political systems such as capitalism propose to establish a viciously competitive deregulated market that has no concern for the people and the impoverished. While planned economies have no place in modern society, neither does the ruthless conflict between otherwise mutually civil parties.

So now there is a dilemma of governance, economically and administratively. If individuals cannot enact their will forcefully upon others dictatorially by virtue of their wealth (as advocated by capitalism), and if we cannot deprive people of the ability to progress in their lives entrepreneurially and keep the social order stagnant to preserve order (as advocated by communism), what can be done?

# The Questionnaire

## Introduction

The right and left political spectrums encompass distinct ideologies, each with its own merits and drawbacks. The right has demonstrated effectiveness in fostering economic growth and innovation, yet it has also perpetuated economic inequality. While the left has shown its strength in providing for the needs of individuals, it has also at times limited personal freedoms and impeded economic progress.

Progress cannot be attained within the confines of either political spectrum. We need to redefine our view of the world to combat the oppression of our current era. This redefinition will require us to think differently about the way we organize our society. We need to find a way to balance the need for individual freedom with the need for fairness. We need to find a way to fix social inequalities while still allowing for growth.

This will not be easy, but it is possible. We just need to have the courage to think differently and to take action. We need to be willing to experiment with new ideas and learn from our mistakes. We need to be patient and persistent, and we need to never give up hope. But what system could provide this?

The answer is Adho-Societalism, an adaptable yet sustainable system of political understanding based on collaboration, justice, and inclusivity. With an emphasis on progress, Adho-Societalism stands in opposition to the traditional ideologies of the past, providing a new way forward. But what is Adho-Societalism?

# What is Adho-Societalism?

As mentioned, humanity needs to rethink its perceptions of the world and fight against the ills of the modern-day to create a world in which all are free, and where every ruler, political or apolitical, is measured by their actions, not their status.

Adho-Societalism asserts that the problem with society is that the two main ways we think of politics and society are flawed, and offers a new, more modern way, to solve the issues of our time.

First, neoliberalism, capitalism, and other such right-wing ideologies assert that the government should be a powerless puppet of the "free market." Communism, socialism, and other left-wing ideologies uphold their position that the market is a fundamentally immoral machine and that the state should make it a marionette, controlled indirectly by its masters. While to an extent, each system has its merits, how they (left-wing and right-wing ideologies) are interpreted and practiced currently, are abhorrent and can only be described as authoritarian. Adho-Societalism straddles the line between these two extremes by proposing measures that tangibly benefit everyone.

Adho-Societalism is a distinct form of understanding governance that can be explained by the meanings of its two distinct semantic parts. Firstly, the prefix "Adho" comes from the Latin phrase *ad hoc*, meaning to do what is needed, and this is the core principle of Adho-Societalism. As pointed out earlier, both prevalent ideological factions, the left, and the right, go to extremes that inevitably lead to failure when either of their political systems is put into practice. These two extremes are the minimal use of the government's capabilities and the constant advancement of the private sector's insatiable thirst for profit on the right. The other extreme is the maximal use of the government's capabilities and the minimization of any non-governmental activity on the left.

With these realities in mind, Adho-Societalism in its purest form is related to leftism, but only because Adho-Societalism sees leftist policies as being able to satisfy the idea of doing what is needed and doing what is right. This idea is not restricted to the notions presented in this manual, but the notions presented here are the purest and truest iterations of Adho-Societalist thought.

# How Does Adho-Societalism Straddle the Line Between Private and Public Enterprise?

Adho-Societalism straddles the line between private and public enterprise by first recognizing that both are artificial structures created to represent the actions of individuals. Such structures aren't machines or computer programs but instead should be thought of as networks governed by those who created them and work within them. However, politicians are not easy people to influence without incentive. This incentive is usually translated into bribery, fraud, and corruption, which leads to the degradation of political structures. Adho-Societalism acknowledges this basic fact of politics and proposes splitting power between the people and the state as a solution to this problem.

While most assume that systems of power such as democracy already split power, this is false, democracy only lets the people decide who holds power, which, while virtuous in its own right, doesn't split power between the people and the state. However, democratization is a way to split power, which is why Adho-Societalism calls for the implementation of omnipresent democracy. Meaning each aspect of public life that requires interactions with systems of power needs to be democratized.

However, it would be best to explain the bounds of this democratization to better understand how the systems of power that exist in our world could be democratized. Democratization in Adho-Societalism refers to creating systems within structures of power that allow those who are beholden to them to have a say in how they are managed and/or governed. The creation of those systems starts with the systems of power that most influence the lives of people. These systems usually do not pertain to the state but rather consist of businesses and other such modes of production. The reason that these structures of power are the most prevalent is that most of the population spends their time, energy, and life working, not governing or voting. Contrary to the philosophies of old, Adho-Societalism asserts that humans are not political animals but rather working animals.

With this basic fact of human nature in mind, and with the idea of democratization, how do we reform our workplaces? One concept of democratization within corporations is the worker cooperative, and while it is a great tool of democratization within a capitalist system, is not suitable for Adho-Societalism. However, worker collectives are a path to obtaining bargaining power without upsetting the owner class. Yet, this shouldn't be considered appeasement since the owner class would still be at the top of corporate ladders, and they would still be elected. How does this work exactly? To start, imagine a group of clerks, who elect a supervisor, then a group of supervisors elect a manager, and so on climbing up the corporate ladder. This creates a system of power that demands that those above must satisfy the needs of those below, and those above them must satisfy them or else they will be voted out. This allows for a market to exist while also giving the workers bargaining power. If extortion is commonplace, the workers will vote for a corporate leader to end that extortion; therefore, dispelling the issues which plague the workplace while also allowing for standard corporate hierarchies to remain in place.

In summary, these alterations seek to create a direct democracy that pressures leaders to govern in favor of the workers within a business.

## How Will the State Be Structured?

The state would be a direct democracy; but its citizens wouldn't have the time, and neither would its government have the resources, to make a total direct democracy (as in, citizens voting on every piece of legislation) possible. Yet, a sub-direct democracy would be viable.

Sub-direct democracy in Adho-Societalism is the idea that while representatives are required, they do not have to be the sole governing authority. Representatives work as perpetual voters, and their vote is unchallenged when deciding on the fate of menial statutes, but when critical matters are being decided upon, the people must have a say. While representatives are not the supreme enactors of statutes, they are the only ones who can propose legislation. Because of this balance of power, both the people and the government benefit from cooperation because if the government puts out popular legislation, they get to stay in power and get to craft its agenda however they please. It also forces governments to innovate and appeal to the people, rather than to large astroturfing movements (artificial/constructed movements masked as grassroots organizing, usually created to benefit large interest groups) and corporate lobbies which usually represent a minority of the population. This makes the nation a better place to live and encourages stability by acknowledging the needs of the majority instead of catering to a small number of elites.

Adho-Societalism also proposes to mend federalism and unitarianism together. How does Adho-Societalism mend these two governmental structures together? Through the power of direct democracy. By definition, federalism refers to a governmental structure in which governmental sub-units, such as provinces or states have equivalent power over their citizens as the central government. Unitarianism treats provinces and states like precincts, defined areas whose governments have no real power and which only serve as ways to make tasks such as the census and law enforcement easier to carry out.

Adho-Societalism proposes to meld these systems together by making local governments powerless without the support of their people. Adho-Societalism proposes a model of the sub-governmental units that are in line with the unitarian vision of sub-governments. Sub-governmental units do not count for representation in a hypothetical Adho-Societalist congress, and neither is the region treated like a mini-nation. But, what Adho-Societalism takes from the sub-government in terms of sovereignty it gives back in the form of the vanguard. The vanguard addresses the claim that each sub-government governs a different set of people than any other and that the laws of the central administration may not be preferable to their citizens. The vanguard is a way for local governments to decide how they want to enforce the law.

The vanguard refers to a bolstered regional government that doesn't have a legislative body since the only laws to enforce are the laws passed by the central government. Instead, there is a legislative body to interpret laws in each regional government. Since laws cannot be ignored, and neither can they be fully enforced across an incredibly diverse spectrum of citizens, they should be allowed to be enforced in a way that suits certain citizens as determined by their regional governments. Therefore, the vanguard is deemed by Adho-Societalism to be the most effective way of disseminating law.

With the idea of the vanguard, the regional government and its people seem empowered, but what about the central government? Adho-Societalism places much emphasis on the rights of regional governments to determine their interpretations of the law.

However, the central government has its form of vanguardism, which can be referred to as central assertion. Central assertion allows the government to override vanguardism by asserting that while the sub-government has rights to the independent interpretation of the law, no right is absolute, and as such, the central government has the right, in the instances of constitutional protection and the protection of the rights afforded by other such major statutes (e.g the rulings of a high court), to override expressions of vanguardism. But only if a motion to do so is legislatively approved (by the central government) and approved by a national referendum. However, since the central government is judicially interpreting the law, an option for a regional government is to appeal any motion, and overturn it or submit the motion to review and interpretation by the state legislative council. This can be approved by the people via referendum if changes are made. However, some elements cannot be changed by the central government so long as they are related to statutes already applied, such as a national or regional constitution, and/or other such high statutes.

Because of the judicial style of legislation taken on by the combined forces of regional vanguardism and state central assertion, we can call the coexistence and co-practicing of these systems "legislative judicialism."

Legislative judicialism allows for the smooth governance of a nation by satisfying every governmental faction's wants and needs. It makes sure that everyone's voice is heard, and allows people to make their own decisions within the confines of their own regions, while also protecting the ability of the primary administration of a nation to set precedents for the country easily and reliably.

# How Will the Nation Be Organized?

As reviewed earlier, the Adho-Societalist business is to be structured as a collective. This collective satisfies the basic human need for hierarchy while preserving equity and fair treatment. However, trying to replicate the collective as would be practiced in an Adho-Societalist business on the scale of a nation would be impractical, difficult, and would at some point suppress equity and fair treatment, the two main objectives of an Adho-Societalist (business) collective, to sustain itself. Therefore, the business collective model of command will not suffice.

A national collective must:

- Maintain economic stability
- Guarantee equity and fairness

- Allow everyone to be able to contribute to the economy/collective

So, what do people need to live and contribute to society? Firstly, people need food, water, and shelter, which is indisputable, so the state must guarantee this to all citizens. However, these are just the bare essentials of physiological existence, but, for people to live a dignified existence and produce value for the economy they must have finances and economic freedom.

Economic freedom refers to people being able to pursue careers in whichever field they choose and to have flexibility in their careers without fear of financial retribution setbacks. It also refers to citizens not being at the mercy of the market, but rather the opposite. The focus is on holding corporations accountable and guaranteeing the common folk free choice in the acquisition of products.

Those products which are needed for sustenance are exchanged in a potluck economy. In a potluck economy, these resources are owned by the state but can be freely exchanged under its guise. The government has the right to hold as much stock of these necessities to make sure that all citizens are fed, quenched, and given shelter, but beyond this, everything else is traded within the national collective. This allows a free market to thrive and provides every single person the ability to make something of their lives and live with dignity. This saves the nation's resources and allows everyone to contribute to the economy while ensuring equity and stability.

# Conclusion

The "Questionnaire" has established the foundational principles of Adho-Societalist governance. These principles include guaranteeing access to basic necessities, guaranteeing stability, and advancing the ideals of fairness and inclusivity. It has also created an economic system that is based on an emphasis on cooperation with a healthy amount of competition. But while these principles address the basics of governance, they do not address the complexities of human nature. So what steps should be taken to address these intricacies?

# The Compendium

## Introduction

For as long as civilization has existed, humanity has witnessed many ideas emerge discussing the preservation of the social order. However, as we soon found out, society couldn't be held together by the rule of law alone, but by creating concrete progress in society's major fields (technology, knowledge, human rights, etc.). This allows every person to truly contribute to society, while also advancing the social order and guaranteeing stability. However, in recent memory, people have been more attracted to simple messages that promise to change their lives and shock-and-awe campaigns rather than the aforementioned ideals of action and progress. But there is no reason why humanity cannot do better and improve itself by acting upon the ideals that it sets.

With this goal in mind, Adho-Societalism strives to improve the human condition by combining the ancient value of producing tangible progress with modern ideas of human rights.

## On the Subject of Progress

Firstly, to progress the condition of a society, whether that society is the size of a hamlet or the size of an entire nation, one must realize the current capabilities of that society to progress and assess its current values. As analyzed by the philosophers of old, human society runs on a constant altercation of ideas, those ideas which prove to be functional survive this battle and are adopted. However, this ongoing struggle can be resolved, a fact that has been forgotten in recent memory due to the perpetuation of extremist ideas.

Every nation should be allowed to act freely and of its own volition and the volitions of its people. The main reason for the strife of the past century leading into the modern era (i.e. the Cold War to the Information Age) is that more powerful nations have the urge to enact their standards on nations without such power, usually leading those nations to ruin. Such interferences sideline the opinions of the people and create repression, caused by the dissonance between the judgment of the citizens and the rulers, with the dissonance usually being resolved in favor of the rulers. For this reason, Adho-Societalism emphasizes the idea of sovereignty, for a nation that cannot rule itself cannot improve itself either.

A society that wishes to better itself then must begin with cultural progress. By assessing their current values and comparing them to their current situation. For example, if a society wants to progress technologically, then it must evaluate those values which pertain to technology. This same rule applies to any circumstance in which a society needs or feels the need to progress. Without the will to change and re-assess social values, no progress can be made, and without progress, the social order becomes stagnant.

## On the Subject of the Economy

A well-run economy is the lifeblood of every nation. A truly Adho-Societalist economy should do what is needed and what is right to protect both the rights of workers and protect the prosperity of the economy, balancing capital and labor.

Adho-Societalism assesses that because all prosperity is begotten from the hands of human workers, whether directly or indirectly, human life and labor should always come before profit.

Adho-Societalists seek to establish a national collective, where all physiological sustenances are sold and bought. Physiological sustenances, as defined by the "Questionnaire" are things that every citizen needs to survive, such as food, water, shelter, and electricity. While the national collective is the supreme administration on the distribution and trading of objects associated such as food, water, and shelter, it also is the supreme administration governing those who labor to provide, maintain, and these resources.

While Adho-Societalism isn't in favor of eliminating a market system, it also asserts the rights of workers to liberty and dignity in the workplace and also states that those who employ these workers uphold these rights. These rights include:

- the right to representation within the business collective (in the form of a union or other representative organization).
- A livable wage on which a worker can afford necessities that aren't guaranteed by the state.
- The ability to challenge those who they think seek to erode their rights.

However, the employer must also be able to propound their rights as well. This returns us to the business collective. To recap, the business collective is a system that functions as a plus-sum hierarchy that depends on a highly federalized system of business elections to keep it stable and achieve its purpose of guaranteeing equity. This system guarantees that those in power (in a corporate sense) reconcile the wants of those who put them in power (through this system of elections). This allows everyone in the business collective to have their needs and wishes fulfilled.

Yet, the government needs to act as an intermediary when the workers rise to protect their rights, and this leads us to the subject of government intervention.

# On the Subject of Government Intervention

The government is the greatest legal entity to exist within a nation, however, this does not give it the right to interfere with every aspect of life.

The government, as an intermediary force, is quite powerful. There are many instances in which government power can and should be used, chief amongst these situations are economic scenarios. In economic quarrels, the government must act in the best interest of the workers and owners alike, rather than the monetary assets in such a circumstance, since monetary assets are both recoverable and compensatable.

But Adho-Societalism also acknowledges the fact that no one party in society should rule over all others with supreme authority. Therefore, the government has no right to dissolve the private market or greatly restrict it in a way that would harm the capabilities of the market unnecessarily. While the market shouldn't be treated as an evil force, it is a powder keg of irresponsibility and greed, which is why Adho-Societalism gives control of essential industries, such as housing, food, and water to the government since these industries could be easily perverted by the private sector.

To summarize, Adho-Societalism supports the existence of a free market but restricts it to protect consumers, owners, and workers from the downsides of the free market system and entrusts control over necessary industries (those industries that provide sustenance and shelter) to the government to keep them stable since free markets rarely are.

## On the Subject of Human Rights

Adho-Societalism acknowledges all basic human rights and seeks to protect them through government policy. But more nuanced human rights that branch out from basic human rights that guarantee a comfortable existence for all must also be recognized. More specifically, most of these more nuanced rights stem from the idea of freedom. Adho-Societalism defines freedom as not just being able to carry out one's will but being able to carry it out without coercion and with the greatest possible capability. So long as exercises of this will not infringe upon the freedom of others and do not cause financial, physical, or emotional distress to others without justification. Adho-Societalist freedom also entails the preservation of the means by which the will of the populous is maintained.

Adho-Societalism also recognizes some freedoms can be abused, and so it should be known that these freedoms can be restricted in circumstances that entail their abuse. Such circumstances include the proliferation of ideas that can be seen both figuratively and literally as harmful. This doesn't prohibit ideas arbitrarily, and neither does it give any party in society the liberty to prohibit ideas arbitrarily, but it keeps the implementation or accomplishment of those ideas in check.

But what are these circumstances that can cause the proliferation of such ideas to be limited? They include, but are not necessarily limited to:

- Ideas that encourage the exclusion of members of society for reasons not based on their character or merit.
- Oration that encourages violence against the innocent or defenseless.
- Oration or ideas that promote (but don't have to outright encourage) the violation of the rights of groups of people for violation of the rules/principles of an ideology, religion, or other such dogma.

These measures only exist to protect the rights of the citizen and the security of the nation as a whole, and if these measures are abused, there must be accountability for the abusers.

# Conclusion

To summarize, the Compendium has addressed the following subjects:

- Producing progress: The Compendium outlines the importance of progress and how it can be achieved. It also discusses how societies can work to achieve progress.
- The economy: The Compendium discusses the economy and how it should be run. The Compendium also discusses the role of government in the economy and the extent of the government's involvement in the economy.
- Liberties and rights: The Compendium discusses liberties and rights and how they should be protected and maintained for all.

Each of these subjects concerns those subjects which relate to our material world. The "Compendium," in laying rules out that govern these things has ensured that these issues and the way Adho-Societalism deals with them are made clear.

# The Themes

## Introduction

Ever since the beginning of human civilization, ancient kings have sought to live forever in luxury, without regard for the slaves who built their palaces. Thousands of years later, we have seen the death of that myth. But now is the time to realize the reality of the human condition. We are all mortal, and we will all die eventually. We must learn to live with this reality and make the most of the time we have. We must also learn to treat each other with respect, regardless of our social status. We are all human beings, and we all deserve to be treated with dignity. Adho-Societalism and through this manuscript, the ideals of a better world will be acknowledged, explored, and expanded upon.

# The Theme of the Human Condition

Ever since the beginning, our kind has forced themselves to accept this notion that there are those meant to succeed and those meant to fail. This assumption is entirely false, and as a society, we symbolically accept this, since we still toil under systems that exploit this fault within our collective psyche. While this has deepened the pockets of those who use the drive to succeed to make us, the working people, their marionettes, it has critically shattered any hope for a better world as well. Adho-Societalism acknowledges this precarious situation exists within all political structurings. Due to the importance of this subject, this manuscript shall explore seven themes that relate both to the human condition, as well to Adho-Societalism, these topics are:

- The organization of a nation
- The structure of a government of Adho-Societalism
- The government's role in social matters
- The rights of people in a society
- The democratic process
- The structure of the state
- The base ideology of Adho-Societalism

But what is the human condition? The human condition is a standard measurement that addresses the quality of a society's political, economic, and social affairs about how they affect the citizenry.

Huge sticking points of any ideology or political system such as democracy and freedom, are based upon the human need for community developed eons ago by our ancestors. Continuing with freedom, that very concept stems from our natural intuition to be able to make our own decisions to guarantee our survival.

Of course, these basic definitions have been enlarged and have led to the notions that we have today, meaning that to truly grasp the concept of the human condition, we must understand all the aspects of the forces that act upon it. While this is a puzzling thing to measure, it can easily be understood once the full scope of the topics mentioned above is comprehended.

## The Theme of National Organization

The organization of a nation is essential to its survival. The organization of a nation also helps us understand the human condition. To grasp this concept, let's examine the structuring of nations throughout history.

Firstly, we must understand that all ideologies and structurings of nations (including Adho-Societalism) only touch on a few facets of human political understanding and only seek to alleviate the burdens of some of the human condition. However, the difference between Adho-Societalism and other ideologies is that even though it explores only some facets of the human condition and humanity's political understanding, it touches on the most important parts. Case in point, when comparing Adho-Societalism to two of the most prevailing ideologies in our history: capitalism and communism, we find many different things. But first, we must present our comparisons.

It is only fair to compare Adho-Societalism to capitalism first since capitalism is the most dominant strain of economic principles in the world today. What is capitalism's main goal? To create a market in which goods can be traded freely and a market where people can provide any good or service any way they want so long as they have the resources to do so. While this sounds good in theory, nothing is ever as it appears. With capitalism's central goal being to create and develop a market(s) where assets can be traded freely, the profit motive soon becomes the main incentive because of its ability to fulfill this goal. The profit motive itself isn't intended to be malicious, but given enough time, unavoidably does by replacing decency and all human morals with itself at the helm of all decision-making. This brings us back to the subject of the organization of a nation. Under a truly capitalist system, the nation is structured to accommodate the central goal of capitalism which is the development and growth of markets and by association, the profit motive. This means that rather than the different factions of society focusing on their roles, they focus only on supporting the profit motive by any means. Any positive progress upon the profit motive supports them. On the contrary, Adho-Societalism prioritizes doing what is needed and doing what is right. So a nation under Adho-Societalism is structured in a way that makes sure that everyone's needs are met and that order is preserved. This fundamental principle also incentivizes the protection of human rights as well as freedoms both complex and simple. This is because social order and human nature are intertwined. People need fundamental rights to maintain their stance of loyalty in society because it is built into us to be free, to be able to say what we want, and hold any beliefs we wish. And while there are regulations on these liberties, Adho-Societalism guarantees a wide range of autonomy to everyone.

This same argument can be used to compare Adho-Societalism and communism. Communism demands that loyalty and the capabilities of the communist state be expanded and maintained to the finest degrees. Compare communism and its system(s) of blind loyalty to any demagogue, which, just like the profit motive in capitalism, is bound to develop in any communist society, to Adho-Societalism, which, as previously reviewed, guarantees all freedoms and allows for free expression and belief.

From this comparison of Adho-Societalism to capitalism and communism, we can conclude that an Adho-Societalist nation must be structured to guarantee the following things:

- The preservation of personal freedoms
- Long-term stability
- Long-term governmental consistency
- Accommodation of the demands of all groups in society

- Protection of the social order
- Preservation of the people's freedom

To begin with, let's examine the last point. The "people's freedom" represents two types of freedom, basic and complex freedoms. While a vague explanation, it can be simplified by understanding what basic and complex freedoms are. Aside from the theory of positive and negative freedom which itself is incredibly deep, Adho-Societalism views freedom through the lenses of simplicity and complexity as well. While every freedom is necessary, others have greater importance in many situations, and so simplicity, in this case, refers to how essential freedoms are. Aside from this, major freedoms such as freedom of speech in and of themselves can be broken down using this scale.

To begin with, any basic freedom such as freedom of expression needs to be guaranteed to preserve order, faith in the nation's collective psyche towards the ruling parties, and the ability for the people to be self-governing. Then, these freedoms need to be kept in check. As ruled out previously, every application of liberty, whether complex or simple, should not infringe upon the utilization of these freedoms by other parties unnecessarily. This clause is extremely effective because it protects personal freedom while also guaranteeing that the rights of others are preserved as well, setting a basic moral framework that is both reasonable and applicable.

While basic freedoms can be easily explained, complex freedoms are more intricate. This is because even though they are descended from basic freedoms, they touch more upon the idiosyncratic parts of societal disposition. Examples of complex freedom(s) are topics such as the rights of animals/non-human beings. The existence of such subjective freedoms only seeks to highlight the importance of the use of democracy, not as an end-all objective, but as a tool to facilitate the rule and creation of law.

But all promises are useless without the preservation of long-term stability and consistency from those parties making the promises. The biggest of those organizations is of course the government of the country and the tool of democracy can be used to keep it stable and consistent.

Adho-Societalist democracy mostly works on forced motivation, this is because power, when obtained, does not bring out the best in a person. Therefore, to control those whose minds have been corrupted by this privilege, Adho-Societalism applies the general use of the democratic process. As reviewed in the "Compendium" and the "Questionnaire," the private market is regulated by workplace democracy, which is an effective tool for workers to make demands, while also preserving the hierarchy of corporations. In this same way, democracy can be used publicly to preserve the nature of society and improve upon it. This does not mean, as highlighted in both the "Questionnaire" and the "Compendium," that it should be used to an unbearable extreme, but rather used in the same way any other governmental service should be used under Adho-Societalism. But while they do sound coercive, "forced motives" are actually positive! This is because when forced motives such as workplace democracy and regular public practice of democracy are fulfilled, those who would seek to personally benefit from the absence of these practices are instead motivated to make concessions in favor of everyone, giving every member of society an equal ability to negotiate.

# The Theme of Governmental Organization

If the heart of a nation is its people, then a government is its mind, and the protection of one is the protection of both. With this in mind, Adho-Societalism affords many protections and rights to the government, both regional and national. But any administration is corruptible and culpable to the demands of the worst of society's fringes, and safeguards need to be in place to prevent this corruption and limit it.

The reasons curbing corruption should be a major focus of any Adho-Societalist government is because:

- Corruption and fraud reflect poorly on an Adho-Societalist government and nation.

- Corruption stands in the way of any agenda an Adho-Societalist government may have.
- Corruption stands in the way of the main goal of the Adho-Societalist ideology: To do what is needed, how it is needed, and when it is needed.

In the case of an Adho-Societalist government, what they need to do is to provide sustenance for their people and work to actively develop and maintain their dominion, both effectively and efficiently while acknowledging everyone's needs. While executing measures when they are needed and when their measures can effectively satisfy the demands of every faction involved. Corruption only stands in the way of these goals, and therefore, any responsible Adho-Societalist government should work to hinder corruption as much as possible.

But, as mentioned before, the goals of an Adho-Societalist government are to:

- Actively develop and maintain their dominion in a way that efficiently and effectively fulfills the demands of all societal factions.
- Provide sustenance for all their citizens.
- Execute practical measures which address and satisfy the two goals mentioned above.

The limitation of unnecessary bureaucracy is also needed to curb corruption. Bureaucracy is mostly forbidden, and this is because Adho-Societalism revolves around the concept of adhocracy or an ever-changing government. This doesn't mean the government is fluid or anarchical, in actuality, it means that while there are established systems of power and there are basic statutes and guaranteed rights, all other statutes and laws are subject to the will of their makers and their beholders. What does this entail?

To understand and answer the question above, we must strictly define what adhocracy is under Adho-Societalism. Adho-Societalist adhocracy is a system of government that relies upon the functionality of legislative judicialism, a concept defined in the "Questionnaire." Legislative judicialism is a form of state-federal contract based upon the principles of central assertion and vanguardism. This is an essential part of Adho-Societalist adhocracy for two reasons, firstly because it is an effective way for different parties in society (namely governmental powers) to command society in a way that reconciles the demands and needs of factions who are commanding, and two because it embodies the true principles of Adho-Societalist adhocracy. These principles are:

- Functionality
- Adaptability
- Stability

To start with, let us discuss what functionality entails. Functionality, as mentioned before is a principle of adhocracy that calls for the maintenance and support of basic statutes and the maintenance, creation, and support of a system of smaller statutes that cover the legal shortcomings of the fundamental statutes. A fundamental statute is a statute such as a constitution, which forms the legal backbone of any judicial and legislative system in an Adho-Societalist adhocracy. Fundamental statutes allow smaller statutes, such as individual laws to exist. To clarify, "smaller" doesn't mean less important in this instance, only laws with a lesser jurisdiction.

With the scaffolding of basic statutes and the exterior shell of smaller statutes, we now have a fortress of law to protect against infringements and set up processes by which parties in society can function, thereby satisfying the principle of functionality.

Now that we have examined the principle of functionality, we must move on to the principle of adaptability. The principle of adaptability carries the trait of the preservation and creation of a versatile system of smaller statutes. This principle sets up a means by which groups in an Adho-Societalist society can lawfully mediate between themselves. This is important since the absence of lawful or civil mediation leads to much chaos in society, which can distract an Adho-Societalist government from its goals and the satisfaction of its principles.

Before moving on to discuss the next set of principles, we must discuss why Adho-Societalism places such emphasis on the non-interruption of these principles. These principles are guides for the function of

Adho-Societalist governments. The fulfillment and following of these principles are essential to preserving the sanctity of an Adho-Societalist government. But why is this relevant? As previously mentioned, the objective of Adho-Societalism is to create a social and political establishment that is dedicated to doing what is needed and what is right. But these two concepts are intertwined, what is right is what is needed, and what is needed is what is right, at least within that circumstance. The non-interruption and prevention of corruption of those who do stand up to this calling are needed to create an ever-improving establishment that is near-utopia at best, and relatively stable and wealthy at worst. Now to review the principles of stability and robustness, the remaining themes to discuss.

Stability in Adho-Societalism seeks to preserve the sanctity of the principles mentioned previously but

also introduces new parameters for Adho-Societalist governments. These new parameters are the preservation and improvement of different aspects of adhocracy, specifically those aspects which truly define adhocracy and differentiate it from other political systems concerning administrative qualities. Another parameter is bestowing upon Adho-Societalist governments the obligation to preserve the methods and processes that allow for the continued capacity of Adho-Societalism to be used reliably and fairly. First, we will discuss the newly introduced parameter of the preservation and improvement of those aspects which truly define adhocracy. Yet we first must determine what these parameters are.
They are:

- Sub-direct democracy

- Circular power division between people and ruler
- Practical incentivization of social improvement measures

Let us start with the idea of circular power division. This is somewhat linked to the social and political incentives mentioned earlier and that will be expanded upon. Yet this concept of circular power division, while similar to the concept of social and political incentives, is not related to it.

With this in mind let's now review what circular power division (between people and national ruling parties) entails. The circular power division exists under the pretense that while the citizens of a nation have much power over the affairs of the state, the entities entrusted with running a country should also have a say in the matter, as it is their responsibility to make decisions. Therefore, to balance the wants and needs of both groups (citizens and state). Adho-Societalism proposes that governmental entities protect systems of voting and citizen decision-making since they have the utmost authority to do so, while administrative systems such as legislative judicialism are protected by the citizen through their action(s) of voting. Guaranteed to them by the protection of this process by administrative entities. This is the circular power division between the people of a nation and its ruling parties. It guarantees that every party in society works towards the common good of all since the means for public conflict are mostly neutralized or eliminated by the guarantee of civil rights.

 In summary, a collaborative system rather than a competitive system is necessary under this clause for it to properly function and this considerably benefits a civilization.

Now to discuss sub-direct democracy. The processes of sub-direct democracy and democracy itself have been discussed numerous times, but these discussions have not surrounded a codified system. Sub-direct democracy is a blend of direct and representative democracy. While that sounds juxtapositional, Adho-Societalism meshes these two seemingly opposing concepts perfectly. A sub-direct democracy is a democracy in which citizens vote on many issues directly, but the propositions which they vote upon are proposed by a legislative assembly. This method is further described in previous paragraphs and texts, which describe the democratic process more comprehensively. To summarize, here are three main components an Adho-Societalist sub-direct democracy should have:

- Balance of power between legislators and voters

- Comprehensive legislative system (preferably unicameral)
- Separation of non-governmental and administrative social forces (e.g businesses and corporations)

With this recap, we can finally move on to the very last aspect of the principle of stability which is the practical incentivization of social improvement measures, which is a broad generalization of several measures. Such propositions include social welfare and aid programs on the most basic, humane level, and continual systemic change on the largest, most administrative scale. This is a large scale of probable propositions to examine. A social improvement measure in this context is defined as any measure which seeks to improve the lives of the general population and is issued by a centralized authority, although this last requirement isn't necessary, it is still important. Centralized authority is any authority with a centralized structure that has the means to fulfill and proclaim edicts such as social improvement measures. Those parties which do not fit this definition, yet still conduct social improvement measures, such as some charitable organizations and grassroots organizers, fall into their own category and are handled by the state and other social entities in a manner that is reasonable, humane, and following Adho-Societalist policy. In most cases, these organizations are a great tool for centralized authorities to enact their measures, and the only instance these organizations would need to be treated as hostiles is if they act in a way that is contradictory to the main goal of any Adho-Societalist society which is to do what is right and what is needed. We can finally conclude that the reasonable implementation of social improvement measures and collaboration with non-centralized groups is a good way to improve society and should be practiced.

# The Theme of Political Representation

While this manuscript and previous manuscripts have mostly focused on Adho-Societalists as an insular group, they aren't. Adho-Societalists and Adho-Societalism exist amongst many other political perspectives and ideologies, and our relations with these other groups are essential to the success of Adho-Societalism, its agenda, and society as a whole. Therefore Adho-Societalists should stress the importance of political cooperation.

Other than the obvious benefit of societal harmony that comes with political cooperation, there are other perks to collaborating with other political groups.

Firstly, there is strength in numbers, and any movement wishing to gain power, such as the early Adho-Societalist movement, needs to increase popular support, and collaboration with like-minded civic movements. Not only does cooperation with other political movements reflect well upon the Adho-Societalists, but it also builds cohesion and alliances, allowing different ideas and different strains of thought within the movement to civilly compete, allowing for further growth and improvement.

Aside from political benefits, a civic partnership with other societal factions aligns with important parts of Adho-Societalist ideology. Civic partnership and political freedom are needed, as mentioned before, for social cohesion and it is one of the best ways to guarantee freedom of thought and speech, in line with the basic mission of Adho-Societalism: Doing what is needed and what is right.

When Adho-Societalism becomes a major political force, its leaders are obliged to pay their dues to those who brought them to power. This means guaranteeing political freedom and allowing every political party to participate in civic and electoral processes.

To clarify, while this text and previous texts seem to demean other ideologies, such as anarchism, communism, and capitalism, this isn't entirely the case. Any mention of other ideologies has been deliberate to show the key faults in them and why they haven't succeeded in matters of satisfying their major audiences, who are usually the people who have to live under the rules of the ideology in question. This does not mean that these ideologies will or should be oppressed and that those who espouse their views should or will be oppressed.

Aside from politics and the economy, another matter which influences society is religion and Adho-Societalists must recognize this. Many other ideologues throughout time have demeaned religion and its role in society. This is a mistake since religion is an integral part of society and shouldn't be seen as a roadblock, but rather as a tool for the spread and advancement of the interests of any social, political, and economic group. Adho-Societalists should not manipulate religion to its means and neither should they shun it, but rather it should respect all forms of religious (or irreligious) beliefs and use it to prove the sanctity of Adho-Societalism in a non-manipulative way that serves social interests and allows for the progression of society positively. Yet the term "non-manipulative" must be clearly defined. A non-manipulative way to serve social interests entails a method to serve social interests that don't tamper with the core elements of the subject which serve the social interests in question.

# The Theme of Adho-Societalist Base Ideology

The ideology of Adho-Societalism has been made clear, as well as its core components, but their elements must be clarified. While the concept of doing what is needed and what is right has been used as justification for many elements of Adho-Societalism introduced in this manuscript and other such works, it still needs to be defined to truly understand the instances in which it has been referenced. The concept of doing what is needed and what is right is present in societal, economic, and governmental affairs. As societal and governmental affairs have been mostly explained and codified, it would be appropriate, to begin with analyzing the aforementioned phrase through the lens of economic affairs.

Yet it is necessary to first revise the instances in which economic affairs have been mentioned. The "Questionnaire" makes mention of a national collective and the potluck economy, although both deserve an expansion in their explanations. To review, a national collective is a system in which all physiological sustenances and their production (water, food, shelter, etc.) are owned and managed by the state. A potluck economy is an economy in which goods while freely exchanged are managed in a collective for each person to freely access, use, and trade without coercion. Coercion is defined as the restriction of economic means. This is demonstrated under capitalism, where individuals *can* make material improvements in their lives but don't have the *means* to do so, trapping them in a state of economic stagnation, and forcing individuals into abject poverty. Adho-Societalism eliminates this conundrum through the utilization of the potluck economy and the national collective, and by providing every individual with the means to improve their circumstances. Eliminating homelessness, poverty, and other struggles in the lives of the average citizen is not only morally beneficial but economically beneficial as well. A nation whose people are prospering also prospers as well. Since the citizens of a nation can improve themselves and their nation and society because their material concerns are dispelled by the state which extends access to these services to all their citizens free of charge out of goodwill and the foresight of the postulation of future prosperity.

# Conclusion

In conclusion, "The Themes" shows that Adho-Societalism provides all parties in society the ability to truly engage in civic life and consigns freedoms and true material gains to the populace of a nation. This is done by acknowledging that every organization has a role to play in the success of a society and affording these groups the means to do their part in improving their country. This ensures that all members of society have the opportunity to participate in the democratic process and benefit from the fruits of their labor.

# Turning Axes

## Introduction

Morality, it has been the basis of critical thought and policy for years, and while important, is the wrong way to examine society. In this manuscript, we will examine the following topics to prove this fact:

- The axes of morality and practicality
- The idea of ideological clichès (such as freedom and liberty)
- The ways Adho-Societalists (and society as a whole) can conquer ignorance
- The issue of power
- The idea of revolution and how Adho-Societalist revolutions are to be carried out

# The Axis of Morality and the Axis of Practicality

In the contest of ideas, most concepts fall into the categories, or axes, of morality and practicality. The theorems of Adho-Societalism mostly fall into the axis of practicality. But to make this judgment the axes of morality and practicality must be understood.

Let's start with the most colloquial school of thought, the axis of morality. The axis of morality is centered around viewing the world as "good vs. evil." While this view is necessary for many situations, it is fundamentally flawed to use this perspective as a starting point for any worldview because it ultimately leads to arbitrary societal divisions and creates insular echo chambers of thought. Which only seeks to deepen these divisions. Not only is this harmful to the society in which these moralists exist but also harms them in the long run by slowly unwinding their conceptions of the world through the evidence of their inevitable failure(s).

Compare this to the axis of practicality which judges actions not on moral significance but on their practicality. The criterion for the practicality of actions are:

- An action able to support a purpose, idea, cause, or other such actions which themselves are practical
- An action that is efficient and methodical in fulfilling its purpose

The criterion for the practicality of motives are:

- A motive that is beneficial to its target demographic
- A motive that can easily be fulfilled without significant or reasonable resistance

- A motive without opposition from the proposers of said motive (motive being a measure in this case)

While these criteria are minimal, they easily regulate a system that is reasonable while guaranteeing the wants of moralists as well. The way the axis of practicality straddles these two lines is simple: by creating parameters that cannot be satisfied without satisfying the wants of moralists and pragmatists. It would be simplest to take two applications of power to demonstrate this principle. The first application of power that will be analyzed is the establishment of a welfare program, while the second is the dissolution of regulatory agencies. Unfortunately, there is no moralist consensus on whether or not these actions are morally correct or incorrect since moralism is subjective and includes moral perspectives both political and social. But Adho-Societalism, being a leftist ideology, considers the former action morally superior to the latter action. With this in mind, the principle of practicality can be applied. Let's start with the morally superior point of welfare. Welfare is not only morally superior but practical as well. The purpose of welfare and welfare programs is to relieve those who use them of financial burdens when it comes to the provision of basic goods and services such as food, water, and housing expenses. It can be argued that a well-run welfare program can support the motive mentioned above methodically and efficiently, thereby satisfying the principle of practicality for actions. But how *practical* is the motive of welfare?

To start, the motive behind welfare is meant to help the poor. As previously mentioned, a well-run welfare program can alieve the financial suffering of the poor, the key demographic of welfare programs, which satisfies the first requirement for a motive to be practical. The next two requirements are a bit tougher to satisfy but can be done. Both of these requirements center around the motive in question having no reasonable opposition in fulfillment and proposition, and welfare is notorious for being a controversial topic with strong support and resistance. Yet this is not the concern, controversy is ever-shifting, but the truth is stable, and practicality is truth. Now to examine the ability of welfare to sway its proposers and the people. Welfare, while still strongly debated, is built on basic principles that are mostly agreed upon and practical motives, principles such as altruism, and without partisanship propositions like welfare are always supported. This satisfies both the requirement of fulfillment and recommendation.

It is simple to examine hypotheticals, but pre-existing morals in society, such as the clichès of "freedom," "altruism," and "decency," should be taken into account as well. These clichès represent essential concepts, and they are misrepresented by the connotations of the aforementioned expressions. While there are many hackneyed proverbs we could examine, we will only review three that fully summarize the intents and connotations. These three ideas are freedom, the power of the average person, and social values.

## Clichès

Three main motifs surround every societal clichè: freedom, the power of the average person, and social "values."

It is wise to begin by reviewing their meaning in the context that they currently exist, before moving on to exploring their actual meaning, and how the corruption of the meaning of the aforementioned motifs has affected society.

Let's start with the idea of freedom. In its trite context, freedom is a catch-all for any action that is deemed permissible by the group/person using the word. For example, many groups throughout history have used the guarantee of freedom to justify authoritarian measures, such as martial law. This is a lie that plays on people's fears, yet, it is an effective lie since true liberty is highly sought after. True liberty is the right of all people, regardless of differences, to have the right to live life as they please in mutual fellowship with their neighbors. Extensions of freedom beyond this definition can be seen as transgressions of liberty because those extensions infringe upon the freedom of the many, while only increasing the liberty and power of a minority. This is a simple codification of the Adho-Societalist concept of freedom, which unlike the trite catch-all previously described, actually maintains the goal of freedom which is to ensure the needs and wants of all people are met in a manner that is reasonable and respectful of everyone's desires.

Moving on to the "power of the people" fallacy which has been colloquially parroted. The "power of the people" fallacy relies on the lie that modern governments are built to serve the people. What is the reasoning behind this claim? To find it, modern Western democracy, the prevailing form of government in the modern world, should be reviewed. Western democracy, as it exists currently, can be best described by the term "revolving door." The term refers to key players in an industry (or industries) moving into the field of politics through election or appointment. State officials exit their role as leaders to become a part of national enterprise with their newfound fame, and vice versa, in an endless cycle. This is the opposite of the supposed goal of Western democracy. Which is to increase the civic participation of citizens and preserve their rights and fulfill the demands of all people. This goal is shared not only by Western democracy but by every well-meaning ideology too. Ideologies are only differentiated by the way they seek to reach this goal and Western democracy is very ineffective in this regard. On the surface, it seems as if Western democracy and more specifically the prefix "Western" is just a formality and that Western democracy is identical to any other form of self-government in everything but name. While Western democracy is identical to plain democracy in many ways, it is different in two ways. First, Western democracy places a high emphasis on the predominance of sub-governmental units such as states and provinces. This can be summarized by the concept of federalization, which most Western democracies exhibit. Second, Western democracies place less importance on grassroots organizing and civic participation and instead focus on the interests of the commercial and industrial sector(s). Growth is interpreted as coming from the upper recesses of society and reaching the lower recesses of society. These two concepts are bound to contradict the goal of civic participation and the preservation of rights because they fundamentally warp human nature and the natural order in general. Growth always starts from those at the bottom, meaning the middle class because those in the middle class have experienced every facet of public life in such a way that they are most able to pass judgment and improve upon social systems as opposed to the affluent whose minds have been poisoned by privilege. The rich only know of the comfort within their marble walls. Therefore they cannot responsibly represent the nation because of their inaccurate view of not only their country, but their world, afforded to them by the privileges of wealth. This very fact proves the practicality of grassroots organization and governance which is present in an adhocracy, the structure of government in an Adho-Societalist society.

Finally, the clichè of social values exists in the modern era to perpetuate the ills of society. As pointed out in the "Compendium" the standards of a society greatly affect its ability to progress in every regard, from technology to politics, and with this in mind, it is clear that the values of Western democracies are contradictory to the development of Western nations. The greatest priority of Western democracy is not progressing towards a better society but the preservation of a profitable status quo meaning that Western nations are run similarly to a cabal: No progress, no intellectual diversity, only a great cult of profit, centered around the economic elite who operate the levers of administration in the same way a puppet master would operate a marionette exists, thereby violating the sanctity of governing institutions and the purpose of a democratic government.

Western democracy is not the only culprit that has committed the crime of violating the sanctity of governing institutions, this is a universal offense committed by leaders of every economic and governmental system. This is an even stricter infringement since Western democracies act democratically in a social sense, yet oligarchic in economic and governmental matters, causing even greater discord within those nations that are Western-style democracies.

## Combating Ignorance

Ignorance is the root of all corruption, and corruption is the root of all evil, therefore, any society that seeks to improve itself morally and practically needs to curb ignorance in every manner. Adho-Societalism defines four forms of ignorance that can and should be suppressed:

- Systemic ignorance
- Trivial ignorance
- Policymaking ignorance
- Social ignorance

Before the tactics that can stop these four forms of critical ignorance from perpetuating are discussed, they must be clarified and defined. Systemic ignorance is the most brutal form of ignorance, and its elimination is critical to the survival of a nation's dignity. Systemic ignorance involves the coordinated disregard of administrators and those who operate systems of power (economic, social, and political) towards a facet of society, such as a group of people or other such association of social elements. But systemic ignorance doesn't need to be targeted towards a specific group of people, quite the contrary.

Systemic ignorance usually develops over a long time, starting by targeting minorities in society, alienated by their differences in immutable aspects of political, social, and biological life from the majority, but soon evolves to the point of affecting society negatively. Systemic ignorance is born of policymaking ignorance, a term that mainly explains the ignorance of the powerful towards the needs and wants of those they hold power over, such as the disconnect between rulers and the ruled. Both these forms of ignorance can be treated as malignant tumors which plague the social, economic, and political fabric of a nation. However, policymaking ignorance is benign in the sense that it can be easily dispelled as compared to systemic ignorance.

There are only two possible solutions to systemic and policymaking ignorance, and those are revolution and political reform. Both of these entail the reformation of society towards a more diverse method of functioning therefore eliminating policymaking ignorance and systemic ignorance by including multiple perspectives. The latter option, while more pacifistic and preferable in many circumstances, is only a temporary solution. Sometimes revolution is necessary, and this is becoming true in much of the world because of the rapid development of policymaking and systemic ignorance and because of the proliferation of these cancerous dogmas across the globe. It is not only individual countries suffering from the doctrine of ignorance, but the world as well. With this fact in mind, it must be recognized that revolution, either peaceful or violent, is needed to bring the world out of the darkness, just as the French brought themselves out of the boot of the royal class, so must this generation be empowered against the oppressors.

But beyond policymaking and systemic ignorance, there is social and trivial ignorance, and just like systemic and policymaking ignorance, social and trivial ignorance are intertwined.

Put simply, trivial ignorance is general ignorance amongst the public about those matters which concern them, but do not have an existential effect on them. For example, a lack of knowledge surrounding matters such as the state of affairs of healthcare, incarceration, or the world at large can be defined as trivial ignorance, even though the issues themselves may not be trivial. But just like policymaking ignorance, trivial ignorance evolves into a much worse form of idiocy, and that is social ignorance. Social ignorance is the highest level of absurdity, in which individuals become so ignorant about the world that they develop close-minded, bigoted, or partisan tendencies and become disconnected from reality.

This has a huge impact on the social and political life of a nation. Social ignorance sows tension in society, and in democratic nations, this tension infects political institutions through elections. Elections are translations of the social attitudes of a nation into its political attitudes. A democratic government is a reflection of the society it governs, and this phenomenon isn't unique to democratic societies, it is present throughout every civilization. Therefore, every Adho-Societalist nation must combat ignorance to prevent the devolution of the nation into a community of perversion and discontent and to continue the practice of doing what is needed and doing what is right.

## The Issue of Power

Adho-Societalism acknowledges the allure of power and how all people strive to attain more of it. Power, in its simplest form, is dominion over an affair. Absolute power is total domination over an affair. An "affair" can range from basic actions, like having control of one's movements and conduct, to complex things, such as sovereignty over a country. The second form of "affair" mentioned is the most present form of the word in most definitions of power. This second form of "affair" is pertained to when we discuss the issue of power. The first form of "affair," meaning control of one's movements and conduct, is defined by the concept of human rights.

The problem with power is that while it is important for someone to hold it, power still needs regulation, but the very nature of power implies that it cannot be controlled. The saying "absolute power corrupts absolutely" may come to mind in this instance, but Adho-Societalism takes a similar, yet different, approach, instead proposing that absolute power exposes absolutely. This mindset isn't unreasonable since, as previously pointed out, a government is only a reflection of the attitudes of those it serves. In this same way, it can be deduced that rulers are a reflection of those they rule. Any stable society follows this basic rule of civilization since leaders who are in tandem with the viewpoints of their citizens can create a society where citizens are satisfied.

But stable societies can also have leaders and citizens who aren't in agreement on most matters. In these cases, the ruling class is supported by the ignorant, and this is the situation in most of the developed world. The ignorant support the corrupt, and the well-intentioned are too powerless to resist this hierarchy. Therefore, as previously asserted, the only solution is revolution.

# The Revolution of the Community

The issue of power has made it clear to us that the well-intentioned are always sidelined. The well-intentioned are those who have practical experience in society, these people usually form the middle class. The well-intentioned are part of a natural community endowed to them by their status, but this community is usually broken by the usual culprits of societal chaos: ignorance and ego. Ignorance separates the well-intentioned by doctrine, and ego separates the well-intentioned by resolve and behavior.

Those among the well-intentioned who realize that they have been divided and blinded soon are faced with the question of how they can solve this problem, and build solidarity with other such well-intentioned people. The answer, as advocated by Adho-Societalism, is the revolution of the community.

The difference between the revolution of the community and other sorts of revolutions is that other revolutions attempt to represent the people of society at large, overlooking the fact that all people are different and that no revolution can represent all people. The community is a group that, while not completely homogenous, is united in the matter of ideology (in our case, Adho-Societalism). This creates camaraderie, an affinity that preserves the distinct capabilities of every person, while also establishing unity. The members of this grand community, unlike the vague group that is "the people," have both a defining characteristic (ideological homogeneity) and a special rapport. This is important since only those who are willing to fight for the cause of revolution can effectively complete its objectives and only a group following the ideals previously mentioned can satisfy this requirement. The satisfaction of this principle also allows for the success of a revolution in two regards. These regards are:

- Achievement of revolutionary objectives
- Achievement of post-revolutionary objectives

Revolutionary objectives and post-revolutionary objectives can be easily defined by the phrase, "the ends justify the means," with revolutionary objectives being the means, and post-revolutionary objectives being the end.

To elaborate, examples of revolutionary objectives are:

- Establishment of provisional institutions
- Creation of measures to enact revolutionary ideals
- Establishment of systems to uphold revolutionary ideals and provisional institutions

Examples of post-revolutionary objectives are:
- Establishment of permanent governance
- Creation of institutions to preserve the results of the revolution
- Enactment of revolutionary ideals

Revolutionary objectives are more temporary, while post-revolutionary objectives are focused on building stability. A revolution is only temporary, therefore, only temporary structures of power are needed as a blueprint for the future of a post-revolutionary world, where permanent governance following the ideals of the revolution should be established.

# Conclusion

"Turning Axes" explores human ignorance and morality, delving deep into the human condition and the complexities that shape our thoughts, actions, and beliefs. It asserts that individual human error, not just collective folly, is what leads to systemic corruption. By examining the human ego, the manuscript uncovers the intricate web of motivations, desires, and fears that drive human behavior and the behavior of entire civilizations.

However, the central focus of the manuscript is not human ignorance, error, or ego. Rather, it is revolution and reform. The Adho-Societalist revolution is a transformative movement that addresses the root problems of society rather than those at the surface. It advocates for a paradigm shift that transcends tradition by challenging people to question their assumptions, break free from conventional thinking, and become part of a community, a revolutionary community since revolution is necessary to create a more just and equitable world. Hopefully, the vision of the revolution will be seen through someday. If not, we will live to see the consequences of stagnation.

# Epilogue

The "Adho-Societalist Manual" takes a close look at contemporary political concepts and their inherent imperfections. It delves deeply into the dominant systems and ideologies that shape our communities, revealing their shortcomings and the negative impact they have on society. It brings to light the challenges individuals face under the current government models while also acknowledging the often harsh reality of their circumstances. However, it does not stop at just criticism but provides practical solutions to tackle these problems. By analyzing and reflecting on the issues discussed, the manual proposes innovative guidelines and techniques for governance that challenge the current state of affairs, recognizing the need for change and action.

The current systems of government are not working for the majority of people. They are designed to benefit the wealthy and powerful while leaving the rest of us struggling to make ends meet. Adho-Societalism is not just a second option, it is a necessary option because without an alternative ideology to counter the destructive movements of the modern left and right, disaster is all to be expected.

But to end on a more positive note, Adho-Societalism looks to improve the world and make it a better place for all. By putting cooperation over competition and progress over stagnation Adho-Societalism looks to embrace innovation, adaptation, and continuous improvement to address the ever-changing challenges society faces. Ultimately, Adho-Societalism seeks to foster a society where equality, cooperation, and justice prevail, paving the way for a better future for everyone.

# Glossary

<u>Adho-Societalism (also shortenable to Societalism)</u>: *An ideology defined by a mixed economic system, an emphasis on adhocracy, and a focus on the well-being of society as a whole.*

<u>Adhocracy</u>: *A system of management focused on flexible and innovative organizational approaches.*

<u>National collective</u>: *A term for the entire economy as a whole under Societalism, where public and private institutions coexist under the government.*

<u>Business collective</u>: *In Adho-Societalism, a term for a democratized corporation.*

<u>Vanguardism</u>: *A system of regional governance where regional governments interpret and enforce their interpretations of the central government's laws rather than making laws themselves.*

Central assertion: *The right of the central government to override vanguardism to enforce the standards of higher laws (such as a constitution).*

Legislative judicialism: *The co-practicing of regional vanguardism and central assertion.*

Basic freedom(s): *Freedoms needed to maintain order and liberty, (such as the freedom of expression).*

Complex freedom(s): *These freedoms stem from fundamental freedoms and relate to more specific subjects (such as animal rights, AI ethics, etc.).*

Sub-direct democracy: *A national system of ballot measures whereby legislators propose laws and people vote on them, rather than just legislators doing both tasks.*

Axis of morality: *Making decisions based on "good vs. evil" logic. While sometimes necessary, it's seen as the lesser of the two axes because of its arbitrary nature.*

<u>Axis of practicality:</u> *Making motives and performing actions based on a list of criteria rather than moralist sentiments. Seen as the greater of the two axes because of its practical nature.*

<u>Trivial ignorance:</u> *General public ignorance about the world at large, a lower form of social ignorance.*

<u>Social ignorance:</u> *The development of close-minded, bigoted, or partisan sentiments among the public.*

<u>Policymaking ignorance:</u> *The ignorance of policymakers to the needs or wants of their constituents, a lower form of systemic ignorance.*

<u>Systemic ignorance:</u> *Ignorance perpetuated by entire systems or institutions towards groups of people usually based on socioeconomic or sociopolitical conditions, the highest form of ignorance.*

<u>Revolution of the community:</u> *Revolution led by a group of people bonded by a common vision and goals, similar to the theory of Leninist vanguardism (not to be confused with the Societalist idea of vanguardism).*